# STARS of PROMISE

The stars of promise shine forth gloriously

amid the darkness of grief.*

- Charles H. Spurgeon

*from *Morning By Morning*. Copyright 1984. Used with permission of the publisher, Whitaker House, Pittsburgh & Colfax Streets, Springdale, PA 15144.

The meditations in this booklet have been

written by parents associated with BASIS*.

Each page is evidence of His working in

hurting hearts through His Word and His

Holy Spirit.

*BASIS - (Brothers and Sisters in Support) is a ministry to grieving parents and families. It is established on a Biblical perspective and uses the Word of God as source for wisdom, love, healing, comfort.

# BASIS

a ministry of Handi*Vangelism
(BCM International, Inc.)
237 Fairfield Avenue
Upper Darby, PA 19082
(215) 352-7177

# PREFACE

"Nothing is harder to heal than a broken heart, a heart shattered by experiences that seem so meaningless. But God's people don't live on *explanations:* they live on *promises.*

Yes, life is tough, but faith can be tougher.

Some people go through the furnace and are burned. They become bitter and hard. Others go through the furnace and are purified. They become more tender and compassionate.

The people who have contributed to this book have been through the furnace. They have seen things in a new light, and they want to share with you what they have learned.

Reading these pages has been for me an experience of both tears and joy: tears as I identified with hurting people, joy as I read what God had done for them, not *in spite of* their trials, but *because of* their trials.

Our Lord does indeed heal our broken hearts, if we give Him all the pieces and patiently let Him work in His way and in His time. I pray that the devotionals in this book will be spiritual medicine to heal broken hearts and turn tears into triumph."

Warren W. Wiersbe
Back to the Bible Broadcast
Lincoln, Nebraska

# INTRODUCTION

"The Lord Jesus took a child into His arms to use him as an example of exceptional trust and faith. How is it that children teach us so much—whether in life or death?

I shall never forget my lesson in trust and faith taught by my five-year-old niece, Kelly, my sister Linda's daughter and a typical tomboy. After Kelly stopped running as much as usual—in fact was limping, doctors discovered an enormous malignant brain tumor. Surgery could only do so much and within a month she was confined to a wheelchair. Now there were two sets of wheels around the big farm table—my adult size and Kelly's miniature ones.

Kelly had so much to teach us about faith and trust. She talked glowingly of when she would be with Jesus, and also ride bigger ponies, eat all the well-buttered corn-on-the-cob she wanted.

The night Kelly died, her mother packed a suitcase with her favorite overalls, shirts and toys. With grace and courage she placed it next to Kelly, who weakly whispered that she wanted to go home— 'Home with Jesus.' Within minutes she was there.

Kelly's death seemed like such a waste, but something was redeemed out of her short life—wisps of wonderful memories along with lessons about faith and trust.

Twenty years have passed since Kelly died, but crystal clear memories of her came to mind as I leafed through *Stars Of Promise*. A short paragraph especially grabbed my attention: 'There are no short-cuts through grief. There is no timetable for recovery. Each of us does, indeed must, grieve in our own individual way and at our own schedule.'

Is it strange that my family viewed Kelly's death as a way of teaching us lessons? For my family our grief was eased in understanding those lessons."

Joni Eareckson Tada
"Joni And Friends"

... I am he, I am he who will sustain you.  I have made you and I will
carry you; I will sustain you ...

Isaiah 46:4 (NIV)

*"Let not your heart be troubled; you believe in God, believe also in Me. In My Father's house are many mansions; if it were not so, I would have told you. I go to prepare a place for you. And if I go and prepare a place for you, I will come again, and receive you to Myself; that where I am, there you may be also."*
John 14:1-3 (NKJV)

In days of grief, many a child of God has embraced, as we have, this special promise of our Lord. Of all the phrases in this promise, the most comforting to my husband and me during our grief are words that might appear to be the least important because they are somewhat a parenthetical thought. Having declared, "In My Father's house are many mansions," Jesus added, "If it were not so, I would have told you."

We have been especially blessed by the thought that Jesus paused to assure us of the veracity of the Christian faith. It was as though He wanted to assure us, "Listen, I will not let you be led astray. I will not allow you to be mistaken. You will not hold on to a myth! It is true! My Word is trustworthy!" In this parenthetical statement, our Lord has reassured us that He will not allow us to believe a lie. We can believe in heaven with perfect assurance of its reality. We can trust the Word of our Lord. "If it were not so, I would have told you."

Several years before Tim's death, we sat in a rear seat in an upper chapel of Canterbury Cathedral and listened to the strains of a male choir. Thumbing through the old hymnal, we were blessed by words written by Richard Baxter:

*My knowledge of that life is small,*
*The eye of faith is dim,*
*But 'tis enough that Christ knows all,*
*And I shall be with Him.*

Rose McQuay
Tim, 23
car accident

Columbia, SC

1

    Though you have made me see troubles, many and bitter, you will restore my life again; from the depths of the earth you will again bring me up.

Psalm 71:20 (NIV)

*God is our refuge and strength, A very present help in trouble.*

Psalm 46:1 (NKJV)

*For He Himself has said, "I will never leave you, nor forsake you."*

Hebrews 13:5b (NKJV)

I know it is the Lord who gives me the strength and the comfort to live day by day since the death of our daughter.

How precious it is just to know that the Lord is always, always there. How many times I've talked to Him and leaned on Him when no one else was around. He always has time to listen when I tell Him my feelings, be they hurtful or joyous feelings. He never cuts me off short or tells me to come back some other time. And, He understands in ways that no one else possibly can.

I cannot imagine trying to make it on my own. I know it would have been impossible to try to live without His presence. He not only is my best "listener," but He also speaks to me and I've never yet had to run His words through my mind to test them for honesty or for how much He really cares.

It is only through the Lord that I've been able to go on and live each day to its fullest.

Mary Genovese
Tina, 15
fire

Williamstown, NJ

3

Praise be to the Lord, to God our Savior, who daily bears our burdens.

Psalm 68:19 (NIV)

*give thanks in all circumstances, for this is God's will for you in Christ Jesus.*
I Thessalonians 5:18 (NIV)

The death of a child is indeed a grievous loss. There is no other loss as difficult to accept, since in our 20th century American culture, children are expected to outlive their parents.

Through the grieving process, however, God's will for us is to be thankful! Is it possible to look beyond the devastating emptiness? What can we be thankful for?

First of all we can be thankful for Christ's atoning death, sins forgiven and that we are His children.

As a loving heavenly Father He sees, He knows, He cares about our hurts and heartaches.

We should take time to be thankful for those family members and friends who have been supportive and who have stood by through the most difficult times, willing to listen and to help in whatever way possible.

And we can use our grief experience, our loss, for His glory as we continue to trust Him and to show forth His love in our lives.

Nancy Beach<br>Laura Mae, 4<br>car accident

Philadelphia, PA

He gathers the lambs in his arms and carries them close to his heart.
Isaiah 40:11b (NIV)

*The Lord is good, a refuge in times of trouble. He cares for those who trust in him.*

Nahum 1:7 (NIV)


It had been many months since the stillbirth of our first child. The devotionals by Charles Swindoll in *Come Before Winter* gave me a specific suggestion that day—to commit the pain and grief that I was feeling to pen and paper as an instrument to aid in healing. I was directed to the above verse—and then to write.

The thoughts were ones I knew and believed—that the Lord is good; He is a Refuge in times of trouble and He does care for all who trust in Him. I had sung the simple song, "God Is So Good," many times before and after my heartache. I had experienced God's care for my wife and myself in so many situations in the past. Yet I still was hurting over the death of our much-wanted daughter.

I began writing—

God, I still sometimes struggle when I hold a baby. I think to myself that I should be holding my own little one; but instead, You are! I am not yet sure how I am accepting it all. I move along, stay busy, try to forget. But thoughts of parenting creep back in. Emotions are released from time to time as I allow myself a moment of honesty with myself or with my wife. I know You are good and that You are my Refuge and that You care for me. I'm sorry for the times I don't acknowledge that more faithfully.

More months have passed and I find the healing process continues. God truly has been my Refuge in this time of trouble. He has exhibited His care for me in ways that I couldn't have dreamed possible.

I'm so thankful that I have a God in Whom I can trust.

Brian Robinson
Lindsey
stillborn

Upper Darby, PA


7

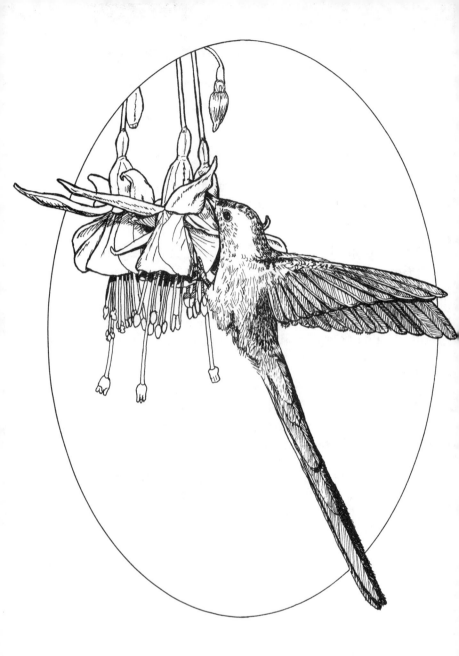

My flesh and my heart may fail, but God is the strength of my heart and my portion forever.

Psalm 73:26 (NIV)

*Since ancient times no one has heard, no ear has perceived, no eye has seen any God besides you, who acts on behalf of those who wait for him.*
Isaiah 64:4 (NIV)

Maybe it is not peculiar to our times, to be impatient, hating to wait for anything or anyone. When we take a look at God's Word and see over and over again all through the Bible, from beginning to end, His bold statements, "to wait," it must be that this is a trait typical of people down through the ages of time.

During my grieving there was a point when God started reminding me to wait. I wanted to hurry up and get over grieving! I didn't like feeling so fragile. I didn't like feeling numb to people and to life in general, and to all that was going on around me.

At times I still struggle with "waiting." My eyes and heart seem to yearn more than ever for heaven and my real home with our precious Saviour. I still need as much as ever to wait on Him for my strength from day to day. And that includes not just spiritual strength, but also emotional and physical strength. How precious to be reminded that if we wait on Him, He has promised us all that we will ever need.

Liz Butcher
Jay, 21
car accident

Othello, WA.

9

"Come to Me, all you who labour and are heavy laden, and I will give you rest. Take My yoke upon you and learn from Me, for I am gentle and lowly in heart, and you will find rest for your souls. For My yoke is easy and My burden is light."

Matthew 11:28-30 (NKJV)

*Therefore I take pleasure in infirmities ... For when
I am weak, then I am strong.*
                    II Corinthians 12:10 (NKJV)


In the eyes of the world, our teen-age son's death was a tragedy. Hopes and dreams for a promising future would never be realized or fulfilled.

Sam was the youngest of our four sons. He was working at a gravel pit when he was caught up in a moving conveyor belt. His air supply was cut off and he suffocated. Death for Sam was a glorious promotion. He was face to face with His Lord.

The world can't see beyond the tragic death and grave, but the eyes of faith know what lies ahead. Sam's life is just beginning in perfection. He is more alive now than he ever was before.

Nevertheless, as a mother who still adorns the human body, I have pain and tears. I didn't know anything could hurt so badly! The absence, void and loss is keenly felt. Yet, I have learned how God can comfort a broken heart. By faith, I am able to look up to Him and let Him dry my tears day by day.

I will have this suffering, just for a while. "For I reckon that the sufferings of this present time are not worthy to be compared with the glory which shall be revealed in us" (Romans 8:18). God uses suffering as a part of His work and for His glory here on earth. What is my little bit of suffering as compared to what awaits me in eternity? Suffering has a limitation. It will not be one moment longer than necessary. God will supply the necessary grace. It's not important that I understand, but trustingly allow God to work in my life.

                              Kathy Guinn
                              Sam, 15
                              work-related accident

Okemah, OK


11

He heals the brokenhearted and binds up their wounds.

Psalm 147:3 (NIV)

*The Lord is my strength and my shield; my heart trusts in him, and I am helped.*

Psalm 28:7a (NIV)

Our capacity for pain is an indicator of our capacity for joy. Our ability to feel is as important as our ability to think. Both are a part of our eternal self, a reflection of the image of God in us. He made us that way, with a beauty and variety that for now may threaten to undo us, may seem more curse than blessing—a risky, dangerous place to be.

We believe God loves us and that in everything He causes or allows He is motivated by that love, and that He has in His mind only what will ultimately be for our best. Reconciling these paradoxical ideas may take some a long, long time.

Three-year-old Jonathan sat beside me as we drove along the highway. "Daddy," he asked, "if I was killed would you still be able to find me?"

Beautiful, bright, Jonathan was the apple of my eye. I loved that boy more than anything else in the world. It was impossible to think that anything other than happiness lay in store for us.

... but nothing I could do, or anything that anyone could do in the next five weeks would change the fact that our beautiful blonde-haired, blue-eyed boy had suffered brain damage through some undiagnosed mechanism. He lingered for awhile, but in early October, when the sugar maples are at their most glorious, he died.

Sometimes we simply cannot know "why." God's ways are not our ways, nor are His thoughts our thoughts. (Isaiah 55:8). He doesn't have to reveal His reason for things.

God can redeem our pain into power. Our faith will be stronger if we can't understand than if we can. [1]

David Biebel
Jonathan, 3
viral infection

Plainfield, NH

13

He is the Rock, his works are perfect, and all his ways are just. A faithful God who does no wrong, upright and just is he.

Deuteronomy 32:4 (NIV)

*Trust in the Lord with all your heart, and lean not on your own understanding; in all your ways acknowledge Him, And He shall direct your paths.*
                                        Proverbs 3:5,6 (NKJV)

Our youngest son, David, was very precious to me. He was quite young when he was diagnosed as having cystic fibrosis. Just hearing the words left me feeling desperate since so few children who have this disease live to reach adulthood.

Like so many others, my first question was "Why? Why my son?" I felt I was a good person. It was not until I accepted the Lord Jesus as my personal Saviour that I realized that even "good" Christian people go through deep trials.

My life was full of turmoil and I struggled daily until I reached the point of putting my entire trust in the Lord. I stopped trying to figure out why this had happened to us. I accepted that God is in control and that as I acknowledge Him through faith and prayers, He did (and still does) direct my paths and enable me to deal with each day.

An added benefit was that David was able to deal with his illness as he also trusted in the Lord from day to day. David was ready to meet the Lord in Whom he had put his trust.

These verses from Proverbs continue to be an encouragement to me and to help me through the difficult times.

Mary Ascenzi
David, 15
cystic fibrosis

Pennsville, NJ

My soul finds rest in God alone ... He alone is my rock and my salvation: he is my fortress, I will never be shaken.

Psalm 62:1,2 (NIV)

*For I am convinced that neither death nor life, neither angels nor demons, neither the present nor the future, nor any powers, neither height nor depth, nor anything else in all creation, will be able to separate us from the love of God that is in Christ Jesus our Lord.*

Romans 8:38,39 (NIV)

The devastation experienced by bereaved parents, indeed by the entire family, is a very special one which can only be fully understood by other bereaved parents!

When our son, David, lost his life in a rock-climbing accident some years ago, we learned many things—among them:

There are no shortcuts through grief.

There is no timetable for recovery. Each of us does, indeed must, grieve in our individual way and at our own schedule.

We also found many helps along the way to recovery. A few of them:

Love was showered on us by friends.

Kindnesses shown us by many folks.

But— our ultimate and enduring comfort came from one source— the assurance in Scripture that our God is sovereign! He makes no mistakes!

How we have rested in the realization that nothing can ever, ever separate us from His love.

> Elizabeth Koop
> David, 20
> rock-climbing accident

Bethesda, MD

Cast all your anxiety on him because he cares for you.
1 Peter 5:7 (NIV)

*... the God of all comfort, who comforts us in all our troubles, so that we can comfort those in any trouble with the comfort we ourselves have received from God.*

2 Corinthians 1:3,4 (NIV)

We just lost our little boy.
After struggling for life through
    surgery after surgery,
He went home to be with God.

He was so small—so young;
How can the void he left be so big?
How can the hurt be so intense?
How can this dull, aching lump in
    my own chest be healed?

I know he is with God.
I know he is well and strong
    and praising God, his Creator, with the angels;
I know he is smiling, laughing and playing—I know he is all right.

But—
I know we are hurting—
    with a hurt often too deep for words.
Some days I try to pretend it never happened—that he never was
        a part of our lives;
But I know he was—and somehow always will be.

Dear God, I need strength.
I need this dull, aching lump in my breast
    turned to peace;
I need to feel Your touch through other people.
I need extra assurance of Your love
    through people who love You.
I need healing—as only You can do it.

Dorothy Gallagher
Jimmy, 3
congenital heart defect

Cherryville, PA

19

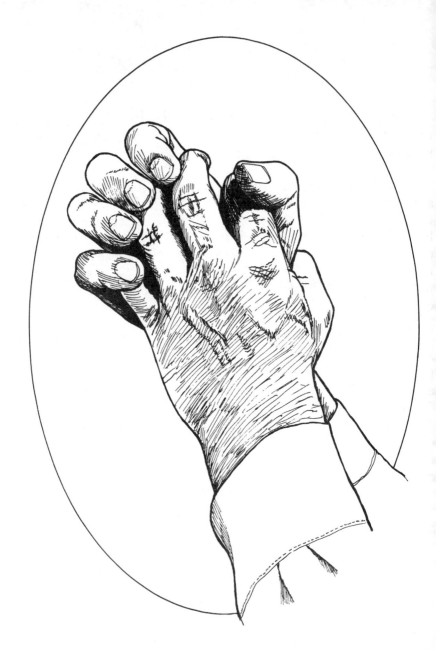

"Hear my prayer, O Lord, listen to my cry for help; be not deaf to my weeping."

Psalm 39:12a (NIV)

How we thank You, Lord, that You are the God of all comfort. We acknowledge that You can and do walk with us through the valley of the shadow because You, too, are a grieving parent.

We admit it is difficult for our finite minds to begin to comprehend such love as Yours—love which sent Your only Son to earth. You knew before there was time that Jesus would be hated, rejected, threatened, beaten, bruised, nailed to a cross to die. Because You are the Omniscient One, You had to know that He would experience helplessness as a baby, and later experience hunger and thirst. You even knew that You would turn Your back on Him and leave Him to agonize alone on the cross as He took our sins upon Himself.

Lord, how can we doubt the depth of Your love? How can we cast aside the comfort that You desire to bestow? How can we not believe that everything that happens in our lives is ultimately in Your control—and for our best.

Thank You that You remember that we are made of dust. You understand our weaknesses. You tolerate our anger and even our refusals to be comforted. You patiently wait for us to come to You, the only Source of real hope and comfort.

We pray in the wonderful name of Jesus, the One so well acquainted with grief. Amen.

Why are you in despair, O my soul? And why have you become disturbed within me? Hope in God, for I shall again praise Him for the help of His presence.

Psalm 42:5 (NASB)

*But we do not want you to be uninformed, brethren, about those who are asleep, that you may not grieve, as do the rest who have no hope. For if we believe that Jesus died and rose again, even so God will bring with Him those who have fallen asleep in Jesus. For this we say to you by the word of the Lord, that we who are alive, and remain until the coming of the Lord, shall not precede those who have fallen asleep. For the Lord Himself will descend from heaven with a shout, with the voice of the archangel, and with the trumpet of God; and the dead in Christ shall rise first. Then we who are alive and remain shall be caught up together with them in the clouds to meet the Lord in the air, and thus we shall always be with the Lord. Therefore comfort one another with these words.*

I Thessalonians 4:13-18 (NASB)

It has been eight years since Mary Ellen went to be with the Lord. When she died, I did not think I could make it through the next month. All I could think of was the time when we would all be reunited with her in heaven.

I was in good health, so I knew I would be around for awhile, and I really did not have a death wish. Consequently, I wished fervently for the Lord's soon return. I was sure I could not endure the intervening time between her departure from earth and ours. The thought of being separated from her for possibly years and years was unbearable.

It is hard to believe that so much time has elapsed. I have not only survived, I have prospered by the grace of God. He has brought me this far, and I know He will take me the rest of the way, however long that will be. Oh, I still long for the time when we will all be together, but the Lord has restored to me a purpose and meaning to life which transcends my grief.

Carolyn Moore
Mary Ellen, 17
car accident

Telford, PA

23

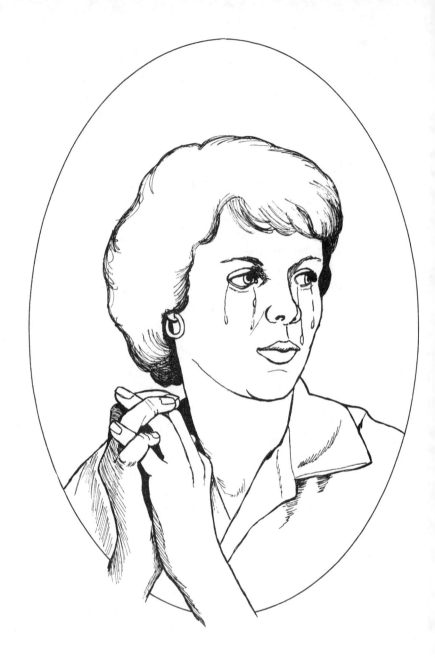

You have seen me tossing and turning through the night. You have collected all my tears and preserved them in your bottle! You have recorded every one in your book.

Psalm 56:8 (TLB)

*"For my thoughts are not your thoughts, neither are your ways my ways," declares the Lord. "As the heavens are higher than the earth, so are my ways higher than your ways and my thoughts than your thoughts."*

Isaiah 55:8,9 (NIV)

*Trust in the Lord with all your heart and lean not on your own understanding.*

Proverbs 3:5 (NIV)

December 28th was to be the first day I would see and hold my daughter, Lindsey, after nine months of her living within me. But those were not God's thoughts. Instead of entering the world to be held, loved and nurtured by her mom and dad, she was taken into the loving, nurturing arms of her precious Saviour, Jesus Christ.

It was at this time, more than any other in my life, that I realized the truth of the above verses—that God's thoughts are not my thoughts and that I cannot lean on my own understanding. I cannot understand why Lindsey had to die. I cannot understand and it is still too painful to let myself ask "why." I cannot discover a single reason that could justify my baby's death. Any possible "reasons" make God look terribly cruel. BUT—I know He isn't. I believe the promises that God gives to me—the ones that seem good to me and the ones that seem not-so-good. I know and believe God loves me so much that He willingly, sacrificially experienced what I have—the death of His Child.

Psalm 37:4 tells us, "Delight yourself in the Lord and He will give you the desires of your heart." This is one of those "good" promises and I know that God has His best plan for me. I also know that I may not always understand or agree with His ways, but I can delight in Him and trust Him for the fulfillment of His desires for my life.

Sandy Robinson
Lindsey
stillborn

Upper Darby, PA

25

Have mercy on me, O God, have mercy on me, for in you my soul takes refuge. I will take refuge in the shadow of your wings until the disaster has passed.

Psalm 57:1 (NIV)

*Because of the Lord's great love we are not con-
sumed, for his compassions never fail. They are new
every morning; great is your faithfulness.*
                              Lamentations 3:22,23 (NIV)


God's faithfulness is without measure.

As sorrow comes into our lives from the death of a loved one, it
can destroy our vitality and the meaning of joyous living. It is possible
that a full, happy, contented life will suddenly become empty and
meaningless. The new void within us blocks out the will to live a full
and meaningful life.

It is in times like these that as we turn to God, He brings to our
remembrance His great love and His desire to share it with us. That
infinite love becomes real, and because of it, we can experience a far
greater joy, peace and comfort than we knew before. It is like the
dawning of a new day with all of its great expectations and hope.

Yes, even in sorrow God is our hope. He wants us to wait patiently
and expectantly for Him.

### Life's Joy

God gives us joy that we may give.
    He gives us love that we may share;
Sometimes He gives us loads to lift
    That we may learn to bear.

For life is gladder when we give,
    And love is sweeter when we share,
And heavy loads rest lightly, too,
    When we have learned to bear.
                              *- Author unknown*


                    Homer & Betty Ostien
                    Randy, 19
                    car accident
Broomall, PA


27

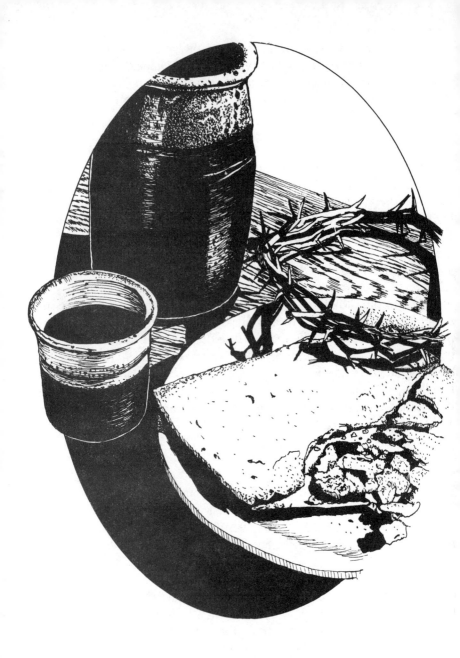

He was despised and forsaken of men, a man of sorrows, and acquainted with grief; and like one from whom men hide their face, He was despised, and we did not esteem Him. Surely our griefs He Himself bore, and our sorrows He carried ...

Isaiah 53:3-4 (NASB)

*...God is faithful, who will not allow you to be tempted beyond what you are able, but with the temptation will also make the way of escape, that you may be able to bear it.*

1 Corinthians 10:13b (NKJV)

My husband and I were in church when we learned that friends had just lost a son through suicide. This young man and our son had been close friends in elementary school. It was a particularly difficult time for them because he was the second son to die.

On the way home I reached over and touched my husband's hand. "The Lord has been good to us! He knows I can't handle losing one of my children," I told him.

Less than twenty-four hours later we received a phone call informing us that our son had been killed in an accident. At that moment the above verse became reality to me! God was faithful and He helped us handle a trial that we could never have gone through alone. He is indeed the One who comforts us in all our tribulation. (2 Corinthians 1:4a)

David had a burden for teens and shortly before his death had spoken of his desire to "give anything" to see teens come closer to the Lord. The Lord gave him his heart's desire as his death made a real impact on those for whom he was burdened. We are privileged because many came to know the Lord through David's death and many others rededicated their lives to the Lord.

A few months before his death, David had written in his quiet time diary: "I can't wait to see Him. I want to hear Him say, 'Well done, enter into My joy today.'"

The Lord rejoiced in David's entrance into heaven.

No, we don't understand, but we know His ways are not our ways.

> Laura Emery
> David, 19
> motorcycle accident

Elverson, PA

I will be glad and rejoice in your love, for you saw my affliction and knew the anguish of my soul.

Psalm 31:7 (NIV)

*I waited patiently for the Lord; And He inclined to me, and heard my cry. He brought me up out of the pit ... set my feet upon a rock ... He put a new song in my mouth, a song of praise to our God.*

Psalm 40:1-3a (NASB)

It seemed impossible that after all we had been through, things would end as they did—with Trisha's death. Fourteen months of treatment for leukemia, bone marrow transplant and it seemed a happy ending would be ours. Now I had to leave the hospital without her, my heart aching to hold her.

In subsequent days, while watching some Christian broadcasts, I heard stories and testimonies from parents, praising the Lord for miraculously restoring their children to health. It was almost too much to bear. I began to question my faith, or lack of it. Hadn't I believed enough that God would heal her? If not, was I then somehow responsible for her death?

As I thought on these things and about God's purpose, I felt the Lord's love for me and a sense of peace and an awareness that it was not the amount of my faith, or the lack of it that determined whether Trisha lived or died. He could have healed her, regardless of me.

It's natural for parents whose children have been restored to praise Him. But for me, for other parents whom God has chosen to act otherwise, our praise to God would not be the result of a natural overflow of the heart. It would be the result of the supernatural power of God! It would be God's power at work in our lives bringing healing, restoring our joy and putting a song of thanksgiving in our hearts. The miracle He has done in our lives is worthy of our praise. It is every bit as much a miracle as raising a child from a death bed.

Each day that passes brings us one day closer to reunion with her and with our Saviour.

Wendy Smith
Trisha, 5
leukemia

Bethlehem, PA

All my longings lie open before you, O Lord; my sighing is not hidden from you. My heart pounds, my strength fails me; even the light has gone from my eyes. My friends and companions avoid me because of my wounds; my neighbors stay far away. O Lord, do not forsake me; be not far from me, O my God. Come quickly to help me, O Lord my Saviour.

Psalm 38:9-11, 21,22 (NIV)

*For I am convinced that neither death nor life, neither angels nor demons, neither the present nor the future, nor any powers, neither height nor depth, nor anything else in all creation, will be able to separate us from the love of God that is in Christ Jesus our Lord.*

Romans 8:38 (NIV)

Nothing—no person—no circumstance can ever separate us from God's love. His love is constant, never-ending, a positive force working for our good.

I may still wonder about God's plan for taking our son to be with Himself at such an early age. How often I think of him as I see a former classmate in a job or profession. What would he be doing? He was a unique boy, full of compassion for others, but at the same time, all-boy. He had a definite determination to have things his way.

When we look back at a loved one's life, we have to be realistic and see the whole person he or she was. This is especially true for the sake of other children. We must not make an idol of the one who is gone so that those who are left feel inadequate.

We dearly loved David. We love him now and always will. He was a vital part of our family. But we must always remember his weaknesses and shortcomings as well as the good things that so endeared him to us.

My desire to help others has grown since David died. Other folks have questions like the ones I asked God some years ago. We cannot understand His "why." Instead we must accept His love and trust Him, knowing His ways are perfect. He is waiting for our question; but that question is not "why?" Instead it is, "Lord, what do you want me to do about this?" He promises guidance as we read His Word each day and ask Him to speak to our hearts that we may apply His Words to our lives and then reach out to help others.

Jane Coleman
David, 13
cancer

Wayne, PA

"... and call upon me in the day of trouble; I will deliver you, and you will honor me."

Psalm 50:15 (NIV)

*Blessed be the God and Father of our Lord Jesus*
*Christ, the Father of mercies and God of all comfort,*

2 Corinthians 1:3 (NKJV)

Even the Apostle Paul became discouraged and felt powerless to help himself. Paul learned to put things in God's hands and to trust Him during the difficult periods of His life.

It has always been easy for me to trust God when everything runs smoothly. Like Paul, I have had to learn to trust Him when things weren't going the way I felt they should.

Nothing in all my life ever seared my heart like the tragic death of my youngest son, Neal. He had spent years overcoming the handicaps of cerebral palsy. He had made tremendous strides and was contemplating marriage to the young woman he loved.

It was only through the comfort of God and the help of caring friends that I started to feel alive again. I also found out it was important to reach out to others who needed someone to listen and to understand their feelings.

When we feel like we have reached the end of the rope—it's time to hold on! God is there, waiting to hold our hand.

How grateful I am to You, Lord, that You have had time to listen to me and to help me. How thankful I am for those friends willing to share their feelings and concerns. Things shared in the spirit of love are the moments we will remember.

Mary Isabel Reagan
Neal, 26
struck by a car

Parkside, PA

"The eternal God is your refuge, and underneath are the everlasting arms."

Deuteronomy 33:27a (NIV)

*... that He would grant you, according to the riches of His glory, to be strengthened with might through His Spirit in the inner man ... being rooted and grounded in love, may be able to comprehend ... what is the width and length and depth and height — to know the love of Christ which passes knowledge ... Now to Him who is able to do exceedingly abundantly above all that we ask or think ... to Him be glory ...*

Ephesians 3:16-21 (NKJV)

A few years ago my best friend died and I marveled at the strength her husband had. I could not begin to comprehend how he functioned so well.

Little did I know that the Lord would show me that same strength through the death of our daughter. We felt God's strength when it was needed—not a minute before. We knew many people were praying for Valerie and for us. God in His wisdom and love took her to live with Him. We have felt Christ's love and the love of our family and church family that He has given.

Thank the Lord for those who are always there with open arms and reflect God's abundant love. No, they do not—they cannot totally understand what we have gone through. They are a constant reminder of 1 John 4:7. "Beloved, let us love one another; for love is of God; and everyone that loveth is born of God, and knoweth God."

When we are grounded in God's love, our faith is strengthened and it makes His love more precious. We can begin to comprehend the breadth, length, depth, and height of His love for us. He is able to do more than we ask or imagine, according to His power in us.

We need to daily claim His power, then God will make our days full and we will be able to reach out to others through His love.

Diana Gotsch
Valerie, 19
accidental gun shot

Timonium, MD

I, even I, am he who comforts you.

Isaiah 51:12a (NIV)

*For I am convinced that neither death nor life, neither angels nor demons, neither the present nor the future, nor any powers, neither height nor depth, nor anything else in all creation, will be able to separate us from the love of God that is in Christ Jesus our Lord.*

Romans 8:38-39 (NIV)

Had Sara been old enough to read, surely these would have been her favorite verses.

Sara suffered first from a brain tumor, then the cancer cells dripped into the spine and she lived for just a few short years.

Shortly before her death I sat beside her. In my discouragement I blurted out, "Oh, Sara, everything is so awful!" She looked at me and said, "It's o.k., Mommy. It's o.k. because Jesus loves Sara and Jesus loves Mommy and Jesus loves Daddy."

I didn't think I had heard her right! We had never used "pat" answers. I don't know how she had such confidence, but her little voice was full of joy and peace. She was more aware of God's love and faithfulness than I was.

Now, years later, I am beginning to see God at work in my life and the lives of others. I am beginning to see that regardless of circumstances, He is there bringing good out of struggles, mistakes, tragedies. He is ever faithful to us.

Yes, everything is "o.k." for those who have been adopted into God's family, because absolutely nothing can ever separate us from the love of God in Christ Jesus our Lord.

Kathy Cupp
Sara, 3
cancer

Pottstown, PA

Carry each other's burdens, and in this way you will fulfill the law
of Christ.

Galatians 6:2 (NIV)

# I Care

In a world where the only guarantee is that
   there are no guarantees;
Know that I care.
In a world where the only constant is that
   there will always be change;
Know that I care.
In a world without hope, true love or
   all the answers;
Know that I care.
In a world where all is temporal and
   nothing stays the same;
Know that I care.


Human love, human compassion, these
   will never last;
But fade and change with time.
The love of God is the only constant,
   never changing love.
He alone endures forever.
He alone is the Friend who always
   sticks closer than a brother.
He alone can truly say, "Know that I care,"
   and mean it!
But—if I let Him, He can say, through me to you--
   I care![2]

Katrina Fowler


(submitted by a BASIS mother)

I would have died unless the Lord had helped me. I screamed, "I'm slipping, Lord!" and He was kind and saved me. Lord, when doubts fill my mind, when my heart is in turmoil, quiet me and give me renewed hope and cheer.

Psalm 94:17-19 (TLB)

*You will keep him in perfect peace, whose mind is
stayed on you.*

Isaiah 26:3 (NKJV)


I was a young girl when the Lord clearly spoke to my heart and gave me the above as a life verse. At the time it seemed like a strange verse for such a young girl. Little did I know how often over the coming years I would cling to that promise and learn that God keeps His Word and makes His promises come alive to those who rely on them. I have experienced His wonderful peace.

And I have needed that peace! A parent doesn't expect to outlive a child and when that happens, even if one knows it is coming, one is never prepared for the gamut of emotions it brings. That is true whether the child is young or an adult.

It has been several years now since my oldest son, John Mark was murdered—mutilated. If it weren't for His peace, I don't know how I could have lived through the ensuing months and years.

And at present I am living with the possible loss of my youngest daughter to cancer. How can this be happening? How does one face it? Lord, again I need the peace that only You can give. My greatest concern is to know that I will see her again. How can I say good-bye without that certainty?

"The Lord gives and the Lord takes away. Blessed is the name of the Lord" (Job 1:21). Help me, Lord, to keep my mind stayed on Thee.

> Lucille Hill
> John Mark, 30
> murdered

Aldan, PA

43

Though he brings grief, he will show compassion, so great is his unfailing love. For he does not willingly bring affliction or grief to the children of men.

Lamentations 3:32,33 (NIV)

*"The grass withers and the flowers fall, but the word
of our God stands forever."*

Isaiah 40:8 (NIV)

One of the most valuable lessons I have learned in my life is that of feasting on God's Word on a daily basis. The more I learn about who God is and His plan for my life, the more I find my eyes focused on Jesus Christ instead of the changing circumstances of life.

When I take my eyes off of my Lord and focus them on the surrounding storm, I feel pressure. My circumstances begin to produce fear and to control me. So it is important to habitually feed on God's Word in time of prosperity, then Jesus Christ becomes my constant source of power and strength. Thus nothing changes but my circumstances.

When our youngest son, Sam, was killed in a work-related accident, God's Word continued to be my source of strength and stability. My circumstances drastically and tragically changed, but Jesus Christ is ..."the same yesterday, and today and forever" (Hebrews 13:8).

Death caught me unawares, but not God, for "...unto God, the Lord, belong the issues from death" (Psalm 68:20). God is always in control and He never makes mistakes. He promised to never leave or forsake me. To know I was not alone soothed my aching heart.

As the God of all comfort (2 Corinthians 1:2) He used promise after promise to heal and comfort my broken heart. But I learned I had to come for a fresh supply every day. Nothing else gave relief. Not temporal things, but the written Word of great eternal value brings satisfaction and inner joy.

I have been able to appreciate the beautiful way God can comfort the grieving heart. I thank Him daily for His perfect wisdom, plan of grace and His promise of what eternity will be—face to face with my beloved Lord and a joyous reunion with Sam.

Kathy Guinn<br>Sam, 15<br>work-related accident

Okemah, OK

But you, O God, do see trouble and grief; you consider it to take it in hand.

Psalm 10:14  (NIV)

The Garden

The garden lay beyond the wall
where briars grew thick
and weeds stood tall.

It was the garden of my life,
old and scarred,
and filled with strife.

But in that garden, not so fair,
a perfect rosebud
blossomed there.

It lifted petals soft and white,
kissed by dewdrops
and morning light.

Just then the Gardener
happened by.
He saw the rose and gave a cry!

"Why that sweet rose cannot live long
in that old garden,
all gone wrong!"

He took it away to a better place—
and left in my garden
an empty space.

Sandy Johnson
Brett, 10
infection

Wrightstown, NJ

Though the fig tree does not bud and there are no grapes on the vines, though the olive crop fails and the fields produce no food, though there are no sheep in the pen and no cattle in the stalls, yet I will rejoice in the Lord ...

Habakkuk 3:17,18 (NIV)

*Now we see but a poor reflection; then we shall see face to face. Now I know in part; then I shall know fully, even as I am fully known.*
1 Corinthians 13:12 (NIV)

We have pretty much come to terms with the death of our son, Jef. Well—at least most of the time. It has come with the help of God's promises of a reunion some day; and with the love and support of family and friends.

But there are still those times—and probably there always will be—when loneliness and despair creep in and we find ourselves again questioning God's purpose in our personal tragedy.

It is sometimes difficult to remember that God does indeed have a purpose for everything that happens in our lives. We would certainly do a lot of things differently with our limited vision. Truly, we do not understand His ways because "... now we see but a poor reflection." How precious is the promise that "... we shall know fully."

Some glorious day when we are reunited according to God's promise, we will understand all the things that are mysteries to us now.

It is not our loss we should be selfishly centering on, but our son's gain in his release from pain, and his arrival at his heavenly home. Even now I can picture him getting ready to happily give us the "grand tour" when we too arrive.

Margaret Wright
Jef, 20
struck by train

Morton, PA

49

"Do not fear, for I have redeemed you; I have called you by name
you are Mine! When you pass through the waters, I will be with you
And through the rivers, they will not overflow you. When you walk
through the fire, you will not be scorched nor will the flame burn you
For I am the Lord your God."

Isaiah 43:1b-3a (NASB)

*The good men perish; the godly die before their time*
*... No one seems to realize that God is taking them*
*away from evil days ahead. For the godly who die*
*shall rest in peace.*

Isaiah 57:1,2 (TLB)

When a friend visited me hours after my seventeen- year-old son's death which was caused by a drunk driver, she brought me the above verse.

This verse gave me permission to feel Nate died too soon. It is natural for a mom or dad to feel cheated when a child precedes them in death. We generally have at least mental acceptance that our children will bury us, but few parents ever entertain the thought they will bury their children. Whenever a child dies before a parent, whether the parent is twenty-five and the child is two, or the parent is seventy and the child is forty-five, we feel the event does not seem congruent with nature.

I also found comfort because this verse indicated God was not surprised by Nathan's arrival in heaven. "No one seems to realize God is taking them away from evil days ahead." God knew Nate was coming and I could rest assured his "early" arrival would be worked into God's perfect plan for Nate and for me. The perilous days could be anything from personal pain to a national disaster, but at least I know God cared enough for Nate to spare him from something worse than death.

Finally, this verse tells me that since Nathan knew Jesus Christ as his personal Saviour, he is with the Lord and at peace. Though I miss him terribly, with the knowledge this verse provides, Nate's mom is also comforted—and at peace.

Marilyn W. Heavilin
Jimmie, 7 weeks, crib death
Ethan, 10 days, pneumonia
Nate (Ethan's twin brother), 17 car ac-
cident with drunk driver

Redlands, CA

Jesus said to her, "I am the resurrection and the life. He who believes in me will live, even though he dies; and whosoever lives and believes in me will never die ... "

John 11:25 (NIV)

*... I know that my Redeemer lives ...*
Job 19:25 (NKJV)

All too often I had heard that if one believed in Jesus as personal Saviour, all burdens would be gone! So when my small son was killed, I tried to pretend to myself, and to others, that everything was all right. Wasn't that what everyone wanted to hear?

But I felt rotten! I tried reading the Bible, but read it without comprehension. Did God exist? Doubts took over my life. Then I read a book by David Biebel, (*Jonathan, You Left Too Soon*) in which the author talked a lot about Job. I took my Bible and read Job for myself. He had many more tragedies to endure than I had. Job survived, but grief took its toll. When I reached the 19th chapter of Job, suddenly it wasn't Job—it was me. It was my anger and depression. I realized it was all right for me to hurt, to mourn, to be angry, to even feel an outcast from home and loved ones. It was then I knew I could go on with life.

Job was honest in expressing his feelings so I knew it was okay for me to let my true feelings be known. And I learned that there are people who sincerely care enough to listen and to be concerned.

How important it was for me to see that Job was still in favor with God after he let all his innermost thoughts be known. Through the book of Job, I've come to know and to understand that the burdens of life are easier to bear when you share them with others—others whom God supplies. I also learned that the presence of trials and burdens in one's life is no measure of their spiritual walk.

I can say with Job, in triumph: "I know that my Redeemer lives!"

Sharon Dawson
Kenneth, almost 3
struck by car

Berlin, NJ

53

By day the Lord directs his love, at night his song is with me — a prayer to the God of my life.

Psalm 42:8 (NIV)

*For our light affliction, which is but for a moment,
is working for us a far more exceeding and eternal
weight of glory.*

2 Corinthians 4:17 (NKJV)

All of our attempts to explain the calamities of life are futile. The book of Job proclaims that we live by faith and faith is surrounded by mystery. When reason gropes in the dark for answers, faith reaches beyond the darkness—to God. God did not give Job the answer to the problem of suffering. But He taught Job the right attitude, that of complete trust in God in spite of all incentive to the contrary. Though we may not understand why our heavenly Father allows us to be afflicted, we trust Him to know what is best for our eternal future.

The word "implosion" means a "bursting within." It is used in reference to the razing of a building through carefully sequenced ignition of explosives. Until I found that word, I had none to describe the human feeling I have experienced in the loss of our son in an auto accident.

An imploded building is not immediately replaced by a new skyscraper. Rubble must be shoveled. New foundations must be dug. New materials must be fixed firmly in place. Human implosion is like that. But for this we have Jesus, Who provides for us "the oil of joy for mourning, the garment of praise for the spirit of heaviness" (Isaiah 61:3 KJV).

Earl McQuay
Tim, 23
car accident

Columbia, SC

This is my comfort in my affliction, that Thy word has revived me
Psalm 119:50 (NASB)

*Trust in the Lord with all your heart, and lean not on your own understanding; in all your ways acknowledge Him, and He shall direct your paths.*
Proverbs 3:5,6 (NKJV)

I have always been a good one for fixing things myself! I like to be busy, to be doing all I can, all the time.

But of course there is no way I can control sickness, accident or death. But He, in His wisdom, controls all things, allows the trials and tragedies in our lives. How often He speaks to my heart, telling me not to try to work things out—but instead just to "trust in Him." Praise the Lord that Jesus never fails.

One day as I was on my way to the hospital where I was doing volunteer work and involved with those who needed chemotherapy, the thought of death was much on my mind. I was also helping at a hospice at the time, so I suppose it was natural for the thoughts of death to frequently be in the front of my mind. I suddenly asked myself, "and what if death comes to your house?" My quick response was, "Get thee behind me, Satan!" But almost as quickly II Corinthians 12:9 came to my mind: "My grace is sufficient for thee." It was just two weeks later that my seventeen-year-old son was suddenly taken home in an accident on the way home from a Bible study.

Since that day the Lord has continued to bring Scripture verses to my mind that meet the need I have at that time. I was reminded over and over again that I do need to trust in the Lord with ALL my heart and to acknowledge Him in ALL my ways.

I live with the realization that my son is indeed "Safe in the Arms of Jesus."

Gail Sell
Barry, 17
car accident

Souderton, PA

But he said to me, "My grace is sufficient for you, for my power is made perfect in weakness."

2 Corinthians 12:9a (NIV)

*Trust in the Lord with all your heart and lean not on your own understanding; in all your ways acknowledge him, and he will make your paths straight.*
Proverbs 3:5,6 (NIV)

"Mommy, who's sitting in the middle?"

"Jesus is."

"But, Mommy, I can't see Him or touch Him!"

"No, but as long as you have Jesus in your heart, He's always there with you."

"Mommy, I want to go to heaven to see and touch Jesus."

Who would ever have imagined that a few weeks later, a healthy young child would have his desire granted? That is indeed when we ask the question, "Why?" and it is also when I am drawn back to the above verses which I chose as life verses when I fully committed my life to Christ.

On the merry-go-round of life with its ups and downs of birth, death, marriage, separation, aging, moving, new jobs and everyday joys and frustrations, it's so comforting to know that God is in control, guiding us each step of the way. We don't necessarily have to understand completely why God allows certain things to occur, but we do have to keep on trusting, knowing that He will allow all things to work together for good (Romans 8:28). Realizing this, there's a certain inner peace that one is filled with—a peace that only God can give—a peace that passes all understanding (Philippians 4:7).

So life's merry-go-round goes on with its ups and downs and going around. But, having committed my life to the Lord and putting my trust daily in Him, I can expect Him to work wonders and miracles and to lead each step of the way.

Lynn Hunter
Georgie, 5
struck by a car

Aldan, PA

Peace I leave with you; my peace I give you ... Do not let your hearts
be troubled ...

John 14:27 (NIV)

*Praise be to the God and Father of our Lord Jesus
Christ, the Father of compassion and the God of all
comfort, who comforts us in all our troubles, so that
we can comfort those in any trouble with the comfort
we ourselves have received from God. For just as
the sufferings of Christ flow over into our lives, so
also through Christ our comfort overflows.*

2 Corinthians 1:3-5 (NIV)

I have a greeting card with this message: "With His great love, our Father will give you what you need—encouragement, peace, strength, hope, and friends who care."

We need to know that is true during the time of trial and grief. If we allow Him to, God will bring what no other person can supply. He will say to us what no other person can express.

God may choose to use another person to minister to those deep needs. Many times that person may never know that they have been God's instrument of special mercy. But I am convinced that as His children, when we are led by His Holy Spirit, and when we respond to His promptings, we will be used much in the ministry of mercy and encouragement. Yes, He can use us even in the midst of our own suffering, perhaps because we are so tender then and can often be aware of ways to minister and reach out to others who are also hurting. Perhaps He can use us in ways He could not use others. In helping others in such difficult times, it helps us, too, in some special, miraculous way.

Liz Butcher
Jay, 21
car accident

Othello, WA

61

Then he turned my sorrow into joy!  He took away my clothes of mourning and gave me gay and festive garments to rejoice in so that I might sing glad praises to the Lord instead of lying in silence in the grave. O Lord my God, I will keep on thanking you forever!

Psalm 30:11-12 (TLB)

## Lord, Let Me Love

He was so young, God,
So young and strong and filled with promise;
So vital, so radiant, giving so much joy
   wherever he went.
He was so brilliant.
On this one boy You lavished so many talents
   that could have enriched Your world.
He had already received so many honors,
   and there were so many more honors to come.
Why then? In our agony we ask, "Why him?"
Why not someone less gifted? less good?
Yet we know, even as we demand what seems to us
   a rational answer,
That we are only intensifying our grief.
Instead, let us thank You
   for the marvel this boy was.
That we can say good-bye to him without
   shame or regret,
Rejoicing in the blessed years he was
   given to us.
Knowing that his bright young life, his many gifts
   have not truly been stilled or wasted,
Only lifted to a higher level where the rest of
   us can't follow yet.
Separation? Yes! Loss? Never!
For his spirit will be with us always
And when we meet him again, we will be even
   more proud.
Thank You for this answer, God. [3]

Marjorie Holmes

(submitted by a BASIS mother)

The cords of death entangled me; the torrents of destruction overwhelmed me. The cords of the grave coiled around me; the snares of death confronted me. In my distress I called to the Lord; I cried to my God for help. From his temple he heard my voice; my cry came before him, into his ears.

Psalm 18:4-6 (NIV)

*... God who gives us life ... is the blessed controller of all things ...*
            1 Timothy 6:13,15 (Phillips translation)


The above verse was the one the Lord brought to my mind when we learned of the death of our son in an automobile accident.

God's sovereignty is the attribute of God that has always anchored my fledgling faith. From my earliest recollection, the truth that God is in charge has stabilized me. Finding my anchor in God's sovereign control, I know that He is faithful whether I understand a given situation or not.

In this world of "wars and rumors of wars" I am daily reminded that "the king's heart is like channels of water in the hand the Lord; He turns it wherever He wishes" (Proverbs 21:1). God's sovereignty is the one attribute that has seen me through our deep grief and it continues to bolster my faith and trust. There are no accidents with God. He was well aware of the circumstances surrounding our son's life on the day of his death. It appears all wrong to our finite mind, no matter how we cut this brutal "pie" of life. Over and over again I have returned to the truth of Isaiah 55: 8-9: "For my thoughts are not your thoughts, neither are your ways my ways," said the Lord. "For as the heavens are higher than the earth, so are my ways higher than your ways and my thoughts than your thoughts."

The reason for Tim's death resides in a realm that is far beyond our comprehension, but we trust the Sovereign Lord.

                                        Rose McQuay
                                        Tim, 23
                                        car accident
Columbia, SC


65

Your sun will never set again, and your moon will wane no more;
the Lord will be your everlasting light, and your days of sorrow will end.
Isaiah 60:20 (NIV)

*"... do this in remembrance of Me."*
I Corinthians 11:24b (NK JV)


I search my memory trying to picture what she was like. I cannot capture the image and it is painful, not to be able to remember. How could I forget someone with whom we spent seventeen years? I torture myself trying to conjure up recollections of her and then realize I am in reality trying to re-create her presence.

As the memory of details dim, trying to re-create an image in my mind could be dangerous. How easily she could become an idol. Only Jesus is worthy of being "re-created" in memories that way. Only He must live in our hearts to be worshipped.

Remembering is His gift and He withholds from me the ability to recall details about my daughter so I will not be caught up in preoccupation and introspection.

Jesus understands my need to remember special details that made my daughter unique. Even HE wanted to be remembered. I appreciate His humanity all the more as He entreats His disciples (and us) to remember Him through the observance of the Last Supper. He knew there would be difficult times ahead when He was physically removed from their presence. There would be gaps in memory. They would probe to re-create in their minds what it had been like when He was with them: His appearance, gestures, speech, laughter.

Memories of Mary Ellen are a precious gift from Him which He allows me to have from time to time — but — only as I can handle them so they will keep their rightful place in my heart.

> Carolyn Moore
> Mary Ellen, 17
> car accident

Telford, PA

I have set the Lord always before me. Because he is at my right hand, I will not be shaken.

Psalm 16:8 (NIV)

*... "No eye has seen, no ear has heard, no mind has conceived what God has prepared for those who love him"*—

1 Corinthians 2:9 (NIV)


"What's heaven like, Mommy?"

Questions, questions, questions. From the time our oldest child, Trisha, was able to talk, she asked questions. For every one you answered, she would ask two more! One of her favorite topics was heaven. Even when she was three and four, we would sit at lunch and talk about what heaven would be like. What would we do in heaven? Would there be toys? Would we play? Sing?

At four, Trisha was diagnosed with leukemia. One night several months after her treatments had begun, she asked me about who would go to heaven. At first I thought she meant people who had asked Jesus to be their Saviour, but she began to list types of people and finally she said, "But there won't be any doctors in heaven, because Jesus is all I need."

Her remark said so much to me—that God could speak to her, just a child and that she had total trust in Jesus, her Friend. I also needed to remember that Jesus was all I needed.

About a month before Trisha died, her questions took a different direction. No longer concerned about what heaven was like, she now questioned: "How will Jesus get us there? Will we have wings like birds?"

Then, as now, I am left with some of her questions. Were they God's way of preparing her for her own death? Trisha now knows the answers, mysteries and secrets which we can only wonder about. One day I will share that with her. For now—Jesus is all I need.

Wendy Smith
Trisha, 5
leukemia

Bethlehem, PA

Gladness and joy will overtake them, and sorrow and sighing will flee away.

Isaiah 35:10b  (NIV)

*For I will turn their mourning into joy, and will comfort them, and give them joy for their sorrow.*
Jeremiah 31:13b (NASB)

We were ecstatic! Our daughter and son-in-law announced that we were to become grandparents for the first time! Three months later our son told us that they were going to have our second grandchild. We were doubly blessed: two grandchildren in one year.

Our first grandchild came into the world stillborn. What sorrow we felt over this loss and the added sadness that our daughter was going home without her baby. "Dear God," I thought, "why is this happening to them? They've dedicated their lives to serving You." He gently reminded me of the words in Proverbs 3:5, "Lean not on your own understanding." I was reminded that we cannot question God's reasons.

With apprehension we awaited the birth of our second grandchild. "It couldn't happen again," I told myself. Two months later we were relieved when a grandson was born. But a few hours later doctors discovered an infection which they could not control and the baby died. We were devastated!

I felt like I had been dropped in a deep pit. I could see nothing but darkness. I couldn't see God's face. I wanted to pray, but couldn't pray—words wouldn't come. I Thessalonians 5:16-18 came to mind: "Rejoice always; pray without ceasing; in everything give thanks, for this is God's will for you in Christ Jesus." How could I be thankful? But the Holy Spirit took over, knowing how much I needed Him. I had a lot to be thankful for: both the mothers were well and our two little grandchildren were in heaven in the loving care of our Saviour, Jesus Christ.

I'm trusting God for His promise in Jeremiah 31:13.

Grace Pelligra
Lindsey, stillborn
Nicholas-1 day
infection

East Brunswick, NJ

> *... He has sent me to bind up the brokenhearted ... to comfort all who mourn ... to bestow on them a crown of beauty instead of ashes, the oil of gladness instead of mourning, and a garment of praise instead of a spirit of despair.*
>
> Isaiah 61:1-5 (NIV)

Arlie and I were dressed in our best clothes, ready to leave. With one last ritual, she opened her perfume bottle and lightly touched her cheeks with my favorite perfume. The fragrance added an attractive footnote to her presence and reminded me that each of us daily presents ourselves with a presence that is acrid or winsome.

Through the years I have become convinced that it is the winsome fragrance that comes from walking with Christ that attracts others to us, and Him, more than all our words combined. Words come as our best attempt to make a statement about our Christianity to others. The success of our words may be little more than rhetorical eloquence. We can say anything as long as we don't have to live it. But the fragrance of our presence as we walk with Christ is wordless eloquence. What Christ does to us and through us, is eloquent testimony to what He can also do to, and through, our neighbors and friends. It is eloquent because it is Christ living through us rather than our statement about how Christ lives through us. I may deceive you with my words, but by my fruits of daily living, you know precisely who I am.

Curious about fragrance, I went to my encyclopedia to learn more about perfume and how we get those fragrances. Most come from natural substances — flowers, leaves, fruits, seeds, roots, gums. But HOW do we capture the fragrances from these things to present them to the world? Moving through the article, certain words leaped out at me — crushing, boiling, breaking, cutting, squeezing, rupturing, distilling, distracting. In each case, fragrance comes from brokenness. A timeless truth leaped out at me — all fragrance comes from brokenness. Is there really another way?

You and I want to present the fragrance of our Lord's presence, don't we? But if you are like me, you want to do it the easy way, without pain or brokenness. I have learned, through the death of our son, Doug, that the ugliness of brokenness is the prelude to the beauty of His fragrance. Like the flowers, leaves, and gums, I must be crushed and broken to exude our Lord's fragrance.

Perhaps you have been hurt deeply. You have been broken or crushed by some circumstance. You can either retreat into yourself and hide — close the door of your life and sit on the ash heap of defeat and linger in the acrid smell of that defeat. Or you can radiate the fragrance of Christ's presence that has come from your brokenness. Was it not that way for our Lord, Himself ? He was broken on the cross, but from His brokenness has come our eternal salvation.

As Christ was wounded FOR us, so let Him take your wounds and hurts and make them FOR someone who needs the fragrance of HIS presence today.

V. Gilbert Beers
Doug, 26
car accident

Elgin, IL

"I am the door; if anyone enters through Me, he shall be saved ..."
John 10:9 (NASB)

In the Bible there are countless promises of comfort, strength, encouragement, healing. These promises are echoed by the parents who have written the materials for this booklet.

His promises are for His children! Are you His child? Have you received the salvation from punishment of sin that He freely offers through His Son, Jesus Christ? Then these promises are for you too.

If you do not know that you are a child of God, these Bible verses can help you:

*Yet to all who received him, to those who believed in his name, he gave the right to become children of God.*

John 1:12 (NIV)

*"For God so loved the world that he gave his one and only Son, that whoever believes in him shall not perish but have eternal life."*

John 3:16 (NIV)

# NOTES

[1]Biebel, David. *If God's So Good . . . Why Do I Hurt So Bad?*
    Colorado Springs, CO: NAVPRESS, 1989.

[2]Fowler, Katrina. "I Care." *Prayer and Praise Letter.* Printed with per-
    mission of Friends of Israel, Bellmawr, NJ.

[3]Highell, Marjorie Holmes. *Who Am I God?* Printed with permission
    from Doubleday, division of Bantam, Doubleday, Dell Publishing
    Group, Inc., Garden City, NY 11530.

\* \* \* \*

Books written by authors whose devotional material appears in this
    booklet:

Beers, V. Gilbert. *Turn Your Hurts Into Healing.* Old Tappan, NJ: Flem-
    ing Revell, 1988.

Biebel, David. *If God's So Good . . . Why Do I Hurt So Bad?*
    Colorado Springs, CO: NAVPRESS, 1989.

Biebel, David. *Jonathan, You Left Too Soon.* (currently out of print)

Heavilin, Marilyn. *Roses in December.* San Bernardino, CA: Here's
    Life Publishers, 1987.

Heavilin, Marilyn. *December's Song.* San Bernardino, CA: Here's Life
    Publishers, 1988.

Koop, C. Everett & Elizabeth. *Sometimes Mountains Move.* Wheaton,
    IL: Tyndale Publishing House, 1979.

McQuay, Earl P. *Beyond Eagles.* Columbus, GA: Quill Publishing Co.,
    1987.

\* \* \* \*

Artwork by Linda McInturff, artist
    BCM International, Inc.